Steganology for the Computer Forensics Examiners

Anjan Kumar Payra

Steganology for the Computer Forensics Examiners

Steganography,Steganalysis,Sterilization techniques for security issues

LAP LAMBERT Academic Publishing

Imprint

Any brand names and product names mentioned in this book are subject to trademark, brand or patent protection and are trademarks or registered trademarks of their respective holders. The use of brand names, product names, common names, trade names, product descriptions etc. even without a particular marking in this work is in no way to be construed to mean that such names may be regarded as unrestricted in respect of trademark and brand protection legislation and could thus be used by anyone.

Cover image: www.ingimage.com

Publisher:
LAP LAMBERT Academic Publishing
is a trademark of
International Book Market Service Ltd., member of OmniScriptum Publishing Group
17 Meldrum Street, Beau Bassin 71504, Mauritius

ISBN: 978-3-659-40336-1

Copyright © Anjan Kumar Payra
Copyright © 2013 International Book Market Service Ltd., member of OmniScriptum Publishing Group

" My work is dedicated to my beloved family, who always encourage me. Like to thank Mr. Imon Mukherjee for his help in entire work. Special thanks to Narayan and Debanka for their help in implementation "

CONTENTS

CONTENTS

1.1.   OVERVIEW:

The word *Steganography* [7] is derived from the Greek words *Steganos* (which means "cover") and *graphy* (which means "writing or drawing"). It is also commonly known as *Disappearing Cryptography*. The image, audio, video, text etc. can be used as a steganographic media. Two aspects are usually addressed in it. First, the cover-media and stego media should be identical under all possible attacks. Second, the embedding process should not degrade the media fidelity, i.e., the difference between the stego media and the cover media should be imperceptible to human vision.

On the other hand, the cryptography [13] is a commonly used technique in digital communication to hide a confidential message using key to make it unreadable for unauthorized receiver. It can hide the content of the message, but it cannot hide its presence. So, the location of the secret message is detectable. This is the reason why an encrypted message can be targeted by the attackers.

Steganalysis [9] is a technique for detecting information from the stego media without having prior knowledge of steganographic algorithm used. Steganology is a very popular field in research that combines both steganography and steganalysis.

Sterilization [11] technique is used to destroy any steganographic information without distorting quality of image. It is very much useful in defense.

The researchers devoted themselves in field of steganology for more than hundred years. Several algorithms in steganography ([1], [6], [5]) and steganalysis ([2], [9], [10]) have been developed during this long span.

1.2.   MOTIVATION:

Researchers have deployed themselves in the field of Cryptography and Steganography. Although both the techniques are used for information hiding, but unlike cryptography, the steganographic technique hides the information in open-secret manner - no key is needed for it. Steganography is a technique of information embedding and decoding without distorting image quality by much. Several steganographic techniques are based on the lsb (least-significant-bit) where changes of image quality are not detected by normal human perception. But it can be detected during multi-bit embedding process. It is challenging to us to embed multiple bits without change image quality by much. Steganalysis give privilege us to detect stego image without having any prior information regarding

4

image except few presume threshold values. Even if we cannot detect stego-media but we can destroy secret information using sterilization method. In my knowledge, there is few such works [11] done previously on image sterilization - that inspires us a lot to design stronger image sterilization technique.

1.3 OBJECTIVE:

My aim is to develop a new steganographic technique which can highlight the possibility of hiding maximum amount of secret information in an image without degrading its quality. I have successfully developed an LSB based, Multi-Bit steganographic algorithms to embed data secretly and an image sterilization technique that can be used to destroy the information stored in 1st and 2nd least significant bits. An image classifier is also specified here simultaneously to detect whether the considering image is stego or not.

1.4 ORGANIZATION/OUTLINE OF THESIS:

In chapter 2, we discuss the background study of steganography, sterilization and steganalysis and their requirements, application, existing techniques. In chapter 3, we discuss details about different type steganography techniques-3.1. LSB based image steganography and analysis. In chapter 3.2, we discuss about multi-bit image Steganography using studying adjacent pixel values of embedding pixel. In chapter 4, content the technique of steganalysis. Chapter 5, describe an algorithm for sterilization Chapter 6, 7 ends with the acronyms and bibliography respectively.

Steganology was also used in both World Wars. German spies hide text by using invisible ink to print small dots above or below letters and by changing the heights of letter-strokes in cover texts. Sometimes critics confuse in term Cryptography and Steganology.

During World War II, the data would hide as microdots. This involved photographing the message to be hidden and reducing the size so that that it could be used as a period within another document. Hoover described the use of microdots as "the enemy's masterpiece of espionage".

A message sent by a spy during World War II read:

"Apparently Neutral's Protest Is Thoroughly Discounted And Ignored. Isman Hard Hit. Blockade Issue Affects For Pretext Embargo On By-Products, Ejecting Suets And Vegetable Oils."

By taking the second letter of every word the hidden message

"pershing sails for ny june 1"

can be retrieved.

When invisible inks became easy to decode through improved technology, *null ciphers* were used. Null ciphers [14] are unencrypted messages that are indiscernible in innocent sounding messages.
An example of such a message is:

"Fishing Freshwater Bends And Saltwater Coasts Rewards Anyone Feeling Stressed.Resourceful Anglers Usually Find Masterful Leapers Fun And Admit Swordfish Rank Overwhelming Anyday."

Taking the third letter in each word the following message emerges:

"send lawyers, guns, and money."

Throughout the chapter , We have concentrated on the algorithm of Image Steganography Using Pixel Characteristic(2.1.2.1), Optimal Embedding Capacity for Permutation Steganography(2.1.2.2), High Capacity Image Steganographic Model(2.1.2.3), The RS Lossless Data Embedding Method for

Uncompress Image Format(2.2.3) , Reliable Detection of LSB Steganography Based on The Difference Image Histogram(2.2.1), Active Steganalysis of Sequential Steganalysis(2.2.2) etc.

2.1. STEGANOGRAPHY

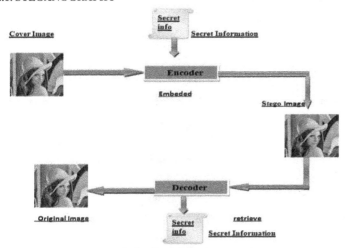

Fig.2.1. Simple image Steganography process

The steganographic algorithms in the spatial domain for selecting the pixels directly can be classified into three groups: non-filtering algorithms, randomized algorithms and filtering algorithms.

A. NON-FILTERING ALGORITHM:

Most common approach of non-filtering algorithm is LSB based algorithm, where sequentially or non-sequentially [3.2] each bit of message is embedded into LSB of pixels of the cover image. As the changes of pixel values after embedding remain almost unaltered. So, normal human perception cannot detect the changes.

B. RANDOMIZED ALGORITHM:

Pseudo-Random number generator is used to generate a sequence key, which is use to access the pixels of the image. By this interaction process and using the obtained sequence key, user can access message in a well spread cover media.

C. FILTERING ALGORITHM:

Now-a-days, multi-bit embedding is very much popular than the LSB methods due to its high embedding ratio or other statistical analysis. A default filtering region of media is selected for designing steganographic embedding regions, which enhance greater quantity of embedding information but not distorting the image quality.

2.1.1. LSB BASED IMAGE STEGANOGRAPHY

Least significant bit (LSB) based [20] embedding is a simple approach to embedding information in a gray scaled cover image. The least significant bit is changed to a bit of the secret message. In case of 24-bit color image each component can store 1-bit of information in its LSB.

An 8 × 3 pixel image can store 72 bits or 9 bytes of secret information. Here given an example to get the method easily:

(11111111	11111100	11110000)
(00000000	00000100	00001100)
(11010010	10101101	01100011)

When the number 250, which binary representation is 11111010, is embedded into the least significant bits of the image, the result will be as follows:

(11111111	11111101	11110001)
(00000001	00000101	00001100)
(11010011	10101100	01100011)

Although the number was embedded into the first 8 bytes of the grid, only the 3 underlined bits needed to be changed according to the embedded message. On average, only half of the bits in an image will need to be modified to hide a secret message using the maximum cover size. Since there are 256 possible intensities of each primary color, changing the LSB of a pixel results in small changes in the intensity of the colors. These changes cannot be perceived by the human eye - thus the message is successfully hidden.

2.1.1 MULTI-BIT IMAGE STEGANOGRAPHY

2.1.2.1 IMAGE STEGANOGRAPHY USING PIXEL CHARACTERISTIC:

This paper presents a steganographic algorithm [7] in digital images to embed a hidden message into cover images. Described algorithm is able to provide a high quality stego image in spite of the high capacity of the concealed information using four adjacent pixels. The number of insertion bits into each pixel is different according to each pixel's values in spatial domain. That is, the number of insertion bit is dependent on whether the pixel is an edge area or smooth area.

Human perception is less sensitive to detect changes in edge /boundary areas of a pixel; it is more sensitive to changes in the smooth areas. Describe method improves on the Chang *et al.*[18] technique by increasing embedding capacity, and we used Thien *et al.* [19] algorithm to enhance the quality of the stego images. Method increases the amount of secret data that can be stored in a cover image, while at the same time producing a higher quality of stego image.

2.1.2.2 OPTIMAL EMBEDDING CAPACITY FOR PERMUTATION STEGANOGRAPHY:

Bogomjakov *et al.* [24] describe algorithm [§3] for steganography using permutation. A statistical analysis indicates that optical embedding capacity algorithm[§1] achieves 99% of optimality when using 128 elements, while using Bogomjakov *et al.*'s method obtain 98.34% of the optimality even when algorithm employing on 1,048,576 elements. In algorithm employed on different sizes of polygonal meshes for the steganography. Both algorithms are described bellow-

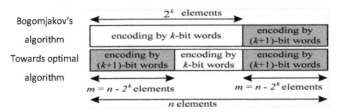

Fig. 2.2. Given n elements which are currently available, our algorithm encodes the first m elements and the last m elements by the (k+1)-bit words of secret message, while elements left are encoded by the k-bit words.

Bogomjakov's Algorithm[83]	Towards optimal Algorithm[81]
Step 1:	Step 1:
Compute reference ordering of mesh vertices into ref[] array	Compute reference ordering of n elements. Place ordered elements into ref[] array
Step 2:	Step 2:
For i=0......n-1	For i=n to 2
$K \leftarrow \left\lfloor log_2^{(n-i)} \right\rfloor$	$K_i \leftarrow \left\lfloor log_2^{(i)} \right\rfloor$
b←peek(k+1)	val←Read(K_i)
if $2^k \leq b$ and $b < n - i$	m← i-2^{K_i}
advance(k+1)	if val < m
else	val← val + 2^{K_i}.Read(1)
b←peek(k)	end if
advance(k)	stego[n-i] ←ref[val]
end	ref[val]← ref[i-1]
perm[i] ←ref[b]	next i
ref[b] ← ref[n-i-1]	stego[n-1] ←ref[0]
end	end

2.1.2.3 HIGH CAPACITY IMAGE STEGANOGRAPHIC MODEL:

An image steganographic model [4] is based on variable-sized LSB insertion to maximize the CE component in spite of adjusting the image quality. Mathematically, it can be shown that the each pixel of a gray-scale image can embed at least 4 bits using above describe algorithm

(x-1, y-1)	(x-1, y)	(x-1, y+1)
(x, y-1)	(x, y)	(x, y+1)
(x+1, y-1)	(x+1, y)	(x+1, y+1)

2.3. 3x3 neighbor position in respect of target pixel at position(x, y)

The embedding technique consists of three major calculations. Those are:

    i)   capacity evaluation (CE),

    ii)   minimum-error replacement (MER)

    iii)   Improved gray-scale compensation (IGSC).

For each pixel, the calculation of CE uses the four adjacent neighboring pixels.

$$\text{Max}(x,y) = \max\{f(x-1,y-1),\ f(x-1,y), f(x-1,y+1), f(x,y-1)\};$$
$$\text{Min}(x,y) = \min\{f(x-1,y-1),\ f(x-1,y), f(x-1,y+1), f(x,y-1)\};$$
$$D(x,y) = \text{Max}(x,y) - \text{Min}(x,y);$$

Except for the boundary pixels in an image, the embedding capacity $n(x, y)$ of each pixel (x, y) is defined as-

$$n(x, y) = \left\lfloor log_2^{D(x,y)} \right\rfloor$$

if value of

    $D(x,y) < 191$ then $p(x,y) = 4$ else 5

The CE calculation perform by

    $C_e(x, y) = \min\{\max\{n(x, y), 4\}, p(x, y)\};$

Next step $C_e(x, y)$ bits are embedded to the pixel at position (x,y).

After embedding, the change of pixel value at (x, y) is $e(x, y)$. By using complement the $(C_e(x, y) + 1)$ bit obtains options for error values.

Then, the MER component finds the minimum error by replacing pixel values at gray scale. Suppose, minimum error is $e(x,y)$. Then, the values of IGSC component will be-

    $f(x, y + 1) = f(x, y + 1) + 1/4 \times e(x, y).$

    $f(x + 1, y - 1) = f(x + 1, y - 1) + 1/4 \times e(x; y).$

    $f(x + 1, y) = f(x + 1, y) + 1/4 \times e(x; y).$

    $f(x + 1, y + 1) = f(x + 1, y + 1) + 1/4 \times e(x; y).$

In IGSC component quality of image is improving by distributing error value (Change pixel value in embedding pixel) in lower four adjacent pixels. So, it remains the image quality best in spite of embedding information in target pixel.

2.1.2.4 ADAPTIVE LSB SUBSTITUTION APPROACH OF IMAGE IS BASED ON THE CONCEPT THAT EDGE AREAS WU AND TSAI'S SCHEME:

In this section, Wu *et al.*'s PVD and LSB replacement method [5] is described for gray-scale images. First, the image is distributed into non-overlapping blocks with two consecutive pixels within the range [0, 255] into a "lower level" and a "higher level" .For example, as shown in Fig. 2.3, the lower level includes range (0-15), and the higher level includes ranges (16-255). Then, select blocks at p_i and p_{i+1} consecutively for calculating difference value (d_i) .Then, determine the PVD range and number of embedding bits (n)   .

◄—lower level—►	◄————— Higher level ————►
(0-15)	(16-255)

PVD Range(d)	Diff. Value	n
lower level	$0 \leq d \leq 15$	3
higher level	$16 \leq d \leq 31$	4

Fig 2.4. Different PVD range and embedding capacity

2.1.2.5 ADAPTIVE DATA HIDING IN EDGE AREAS OF IMAGES WITH SPATIAL LSB DOMAIN SYSTEMS:

This paper proposes a new adaptive least-significant bit (LSB) steganographic method [6] using pixel-value differencing (PVD) that provides a larger embedding capacity but variation of quality of stego image is imperceptible. The method calculates the difference value of two consecutive pixels to estimate how many secret bits will be embedded into the two pixels. Pixels located in the edge areas are embedded by a n-bit LSB substitution method .The PVD values partition the total range (0 to 255) into lower level (0 to 15), middle level (16 to 31), and higher level(32 to255). Thus any pair of adjacent pixels can embed by n^{th} bits using LSB substitution methods.

It is determined by the level which the difference value belongs to. Before and after embedding the PVD values of two consecutive pixels should remain in same range otherwise we require to performing adjustment in spatial domain.

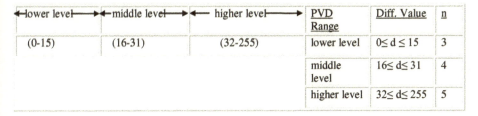

← lower level →	← middle level →	← higher level →	PVD Range	Diff. Value	n
(0-15)	(16-31)	(32-255)	lower level	$0 \leq d \leq 15$	3
			middle level	$16 \leq d \leq 31$	4
			higher level	$32 \leq d \leq 255$	5

Fig 2.5. Different PVD range and embedding capacity

2.2   STEGANALYSIS :

2.2.1 RELIABLE DETECTION OF LSB STEGANOGRAPHY BASED ON THE DIFFERENCE IMAGE HISTOGRAM:

The steganalysis technique [8] based on the difference image histogram for LSB steganographic technique is used. Suppose, the cover image (I) with dimension M X N, then maximum data hiding using LSB steganography M X N. If e_{em} is embedded bits and maximum embeddable bit is e_m. If p is embedding ratio, then $p = e_{em}/e_m \times 100$.

Translation coefficients (p) between difference image histograms are used as a correlation between the least significant bit (LSB) plane and the remained bit planes, and then it is used to differentiate the stego-image from the cover image. The algorithm can obtain existence, length of the information in the stego image. Results prove that it is better than RS analysis method and improves the computation speed significantly. Steganalysis is also used for evaluating, identifying the weaknesses and improving the security of steganographic systems. A method based on statistical analysis of Pairs of Values (PoVs) that are exchanged during message embedding [1]. This method provides very reliable results for steganography based on sequential LSB replacement. RS analysis is an effective steganalytic technique recently proposed by Fridrich et.al. [10]. by considering the threshold values, we can obtain different histograms for cover and stego image which can use to detect stego and carrier image.

2.2.2 ACTIVE STEGANALYSIS OF SEQUENTIAL STEGANALYSIS OF IMAGE:

The objective of steganalysis [9] is to break steganographic tool, information, position of information and length of the information. A steganalysis detector attempts to detect the presence/absence of an embedded message when presented with a stego signal. We classify steganalysis into two general categories: (a) *passive* and (b) *active*.

Passive steganalysis deals with:

- Detect presence/absence of hidden message in a stego signal.
- Identify the stego embedding algorithm

While active steganalysis deals with the following:

- Estimate the embedded message length.
- Estimate location(s) of the hidden message.
- Estimate the secret key used in embedding.
- Estimate some parameters of the stego embedding algorithm.
- Extract the hidden message.

Sequential steganography is used here as the stenographic algorithm. Example of sequential steganography:

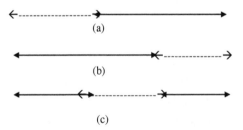

(a)

(b)

(c)

Figure 2.6. Example scenarios of different type sequential steganography ((a),(b),(c)). Dotted lines indicate locations where a message is embedded

One of the mathematical tools that we employ to detect the changes in statistics of an observed signal (stochastic process) is the sequential probability ratio test. As a result, a cumulative sum (CUSUM) test statistic is derived for detecting change points in the observed stochastic process.

Other Steganalysis algorithm like J. Fridrich, M. Goljan, R. Du-" Lossless Data Embedding For All Image Formats"[10], J.Zhang and hu,Yuan-"Detection of LSB matching using the envelope of histogram", F. Huang, B. Li, J. Huang-" Attack Lsb Matching Steganography By Counting Alteration Rate Of The Number Of Neighbourhood Gray Levels"[20] focus on new ray as forensic tools.

2.3 STERILIZATION

Sterilization is an important forensic examiner's tool in field of biomedical and defense or in security domain. It is first time use in the image processing .If steganalysis is not able to detect anti forensic tools or decode information from suspected image ,then sterilization shows it's strong participation. Suppose, examiner detects a suspicious medium or network, then it is not requiring to block permission of access or to know steganography algorithm.

In bitmap image, image consist three color planes. They are red, green and blue color components. One of the most popular steganography techniques is Least Significant Bit (LSB) insertion. Typically, there are thousands of pixels in an image. So if we change the LSB of some pixels, the resulting picture will probably be alike to the original image.

$$MSB = 2^7 = 128$$
$$LSB = 2^0 = 1$$

The LSB flipping function for a stego image is defined by $F1 = 0 \leftrightarrow 1, 2 \leftrightarrow 3, 4 \leftrightarrow 5......48 \leftrightarrow 49....254 \leftrightarrow 255$ etc. The groups are formed based on this flipping function. The intensity values $2s$ (even) and $2s+1$(odd), for $0 \leq j \leq 127$, belong to the same group. So the maximum possible number of groups for each component of an image is 128.

For example suppose,
$$75_{10} = 100101\boxed{1}$$

$$74_{10} = 100101\boxed{0}$$

So, 74_{10} and 75_{10} form a group.

Suppose that an image contains N pixels with c groups. Let n_i be the number of pixels in the ith group, $1 \leq i \leq c$. Thus, count value $N = \Sigma\, n_i$ The set of pixels (based on their intensity values) for the ith group is represented by $G_i = \{x_{i,k}: 1 \leq k \leq ni\}$, such that $x_{i,j} - x_{i,m} \in \{-1, 0, +1\}$, $1 \leq j \neq m \leq n_i$.

The sterilization algorithm is [11]-Our objective is to obtain sterilized image using describe algorithm as given bellow. Operation is performed in spatial domain. Study intensity values from input stego image. The LSB values of pixel of stego image are flipped. Gather in groups based on the pixel values. Estimate the count of odd and even pixels in form of (2s+1) and 2s respectively. Suppose, n_o and n_e are the odd and even count respectively. If $n_e > n_o$ then replace all 2s+1 by 2s, else replace 2s values by 2s+1.

The given approaches have to continue for all three components in RGB model images. Those are discussed in latter sections.

3. 1 LSB BASED IMAGE STEGANOGRAPHY

We know that the gray scale image pixel consists of 8 bits. That means it has 2^8 different color levels. So, different between two consecutive color levels does not perceptible in normal human eyes. Thus, if we change the least bit of a pixel of gray scale image then the quality of image remains almost same. Using this phenomena ,the LSB based steganographic algorithm become popular.

3.1.1 SEQUENTIAL STEGANOGRAPHIC ALGORITHM:

A. EMBEDDING:

Step 1: Read given image pixel values and Secret information.

Step 2: Convert each character of Secret information into binary form with at least 8 bits.

Step 4: Set LSB of pixel values by corresponding 0 and 1 taking from binary representation of secret message in sequential manner.

Step 5: Repeat step 4 until information bit remains.

Step 6: Stop

B. RETRIEVING:

Step 1: Select one pixel from the stego image.

Step 2: Fetch the LSB of the pixel and append it into binary form with at least 8 bits.

Step 3: Repeat Step 1 and Step 2 until information remain.

Step 4: Numeric matrix converted into string. Obtain the desire hidden information.

Step 5: Display results.

Step 6: End

Above given algorithms (embedding & retrieving) are quit easy and simple. Here select lsb bit of cover image during embedding to embed secrete information. Similarly, at receiver side it receive stego image and select lsb of stego image and decrypt or retrieve the secrete information. The algorithms are applied over several images. The results are discussed and analysis below-

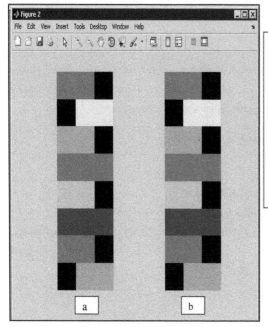

Caesar was born into a patrician family, the *gens Julia*, which claimed descent from Iulus, son of the legendary Trojan prince Aeneas, supposedly the son of the goddess Venus.

c

a   b

Fig3.1: (a) sample.bmp(before embedding)
(b) sample_stego.bmp(after embedding)
(c) inserted text [22]

Embed secret information as given in Fig3.1: (c) using sequential lsb embedding algorithm, we obtain images as given in Fig3.1: (a) and Fig3.1: (b). The differences between cover and stego images can't be detected by normal human vision. Only analysis tools (as like – histogram and pixel value differencing) can detect it. So, those are given below-

C) HISTOGRAM ANALYSIS:

Histogram [21] is a statistical, graphical measurement of the image. It counts occurrence of disjoint sets of pixels values in image and other operations like probability density function, cumulative sum. Histogram of a digital image with intensity levels in the range [0, L-1] is a discrete function $h(r_k) = n_k$, where r_k is the kth intensity value and n_k is the number of pixels in the image with intensity r_k.

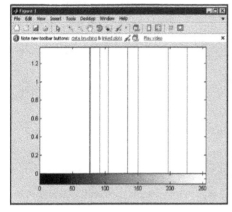
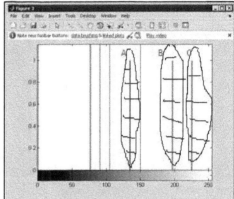

Histogram of red component of sample.bmp   Histogram of red component of sample_stego.bmp

Fig 3.2. Histogram study for sample.bmp and sample_stego.bmp.

As histogram analysis is given above, clearly changes of values are located in figure by three main regions (A, B, C). So, analytical tools are always important tool to judge an image is stego or cover image.

D) PVD ANALYSIS:

It is an analysis based on spatial domain of a given image. Here we consider pixel values cover image (sample.bmp) and stego image (sample_stego.bmp) and try to find differences between them.

The Pixel Value Difference (PVD) is determined by:

$$pvd_{i,j} = c_{i,j} - s_{i,j}$$, where $c_{i,j}$ is the pixel value of red component of the cover image

at (i,j) position

and $s_{i,j}$ is the pixel value of red component of the stego image

at (i,j) position.

It is quite obvious that pixel values of cover and stego images should be changed. This approach can also useful to distinguish between cover and stego images. Pixel values differences of sample_stego.bmp images are marked in red.

19

sample.bmp			sample_stego.bmp		
255	255	0	254	254	0
0	255	255	0	255	254
1	1	0	1	0	1
254	254	254	254	254	254
167	167	0	166	167	0
129	129	129	128	128	128
236	236	0	236	236	0
0	1	1	0	1	0

Table 3.1: Pixel values of red component of cover image (sample.bmp) and stego image (sample_stego.bmp)

Since Table 3.1 shows that the $pvd_{i,j} \in \{-1, 0, +1\}$, thus changes between both images cannot be visualize by human eye.

3.1.2 MATRIX BASED STEGANOGRAPHIC ALGORITHM :

A) EMBEDDING PROCESS:

Step 1: Read given image pixel values & Secret information.

Step 2: Convert each character of Secret information into binary and transpose it

Step 3: Calculate position of zero & one in transpose matrix of Secret Information. Save position indexes

      in matrixes.

Step 4: Set LSB of pixel values by corresponding zero & ones with indices respectively.

Step 5: Repeat step 4 until information bit remains.

Step 6: End

B) EXTRACTION PROCESS:

Step 1: To retrieve the secret information, extract the LSB from stego image.

Step 2: Numeric matrix converted into string. Obtain the desire hidden information.

Step 3: Display results. It is end of LSB steganography.

EXAMPLE:
Above algorithm apply on c.bmp image and obtain following result.

Pixel values of red component of image sample.bmp

255	255	0
0	255	255
1	1	0
254	254	254
167	167	0
129	129	129
236	236	0
0	1	1

To explain the technique clearly, we have here considered 6 byte of information for a sample small image. Following are the position of zero in information matrix-

1   2   4   5   8   9   11   12   17   18   20   21   22   23   24

Following position of one in information is –

3   6   7   10   13   14   15   16   19

After embedding, the pixel values of red component of stego image are-

sample.bmp			sample_stego.bmp		
255	255	0	254	254	0
0	255	255	0	255	254
1	1	0	1	0	1
254	254	254	254	254	254
167	167	0	166	167	0
129	129	129	129	129	128
236	236	0	237	237	0
0	1	1	0	1	0

Table 3.2. Result study for non sequential LSB image Steganography.

We have applied above describe algorithm on lena.bmp and secret information is embedded in it. Characteristics of results obtained using propose algorithm are given bellow,

Caesar left Rome and joined the army, where he wor
the Civic Crown for his part in an important siege. On a
mission to Bithynia to secure the assistance of King
Nicomedes's fleet, he spent so long at his court that
rumours of an affair with the king arose, which Caesa
would vehemently deny for the rest of his life
Ironically, the loss of his priesthood had allowed him
to pursue a military career: the high priest of Jupite
was not permitted to touch a horse, sleep three night
outside his own bed or one night outside Rome, o
look upon an army.

(a)   (b)

Fig3.3. (a) Lena.bmp (before embedding)   (b) Secret information [22]

After embedding, we display both cover and stego image in subplots. 1st one represent cover image
and 2nd one represent stego image. After decoding (extraction), secret information display in command
window. Result is given below,

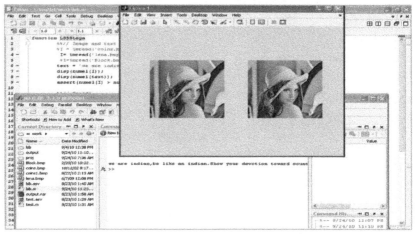

Fig 3.4 Results of LSB algorithm

22

Applying above said algorithm on lena.bmp and coins.bmp and gets following results:

Fig 3.5. Cover image of lena.bmp, coins.bmp and their stego image respectively.

C) HISTOGRAM ANALYSIS:

Histogram of lena.bmp and LenaStego.bmp image are given bellow. The differences between the cover and stego images are not clearly visible due to large number of pixels.

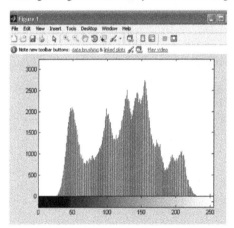 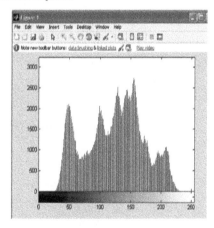

Fig .3.6 Studying histogram lena.bmp and LenaStego.bmp

Differentiation is not detected in histograms using LSB embedding procedure as the changes of pixel values are restricted with in (-1, 0, 1).

23

D) PVD ANALYSIS:

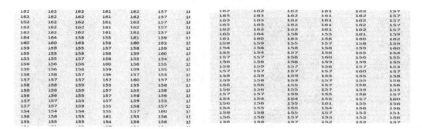

Fig 3.7 Studying pixel values for lena.bmp and LenaStego.bmp

But by studying pixel value analysis, the changes between cover and stego images are clearly visible. Even we can generate PVD matrix.

E) BIT-PLANE ANALYSIS

The intensity of each pixel in 256-level gray-scale image is composed 8-bits.By isolating particular bits of the pixel values in an image we can highlight interesting aspects of that image. Higher-order bits usually contain most of the significant visual information Lower-order bits contain subtle details.

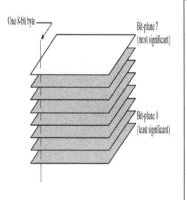

Fig 3.7 Bit-plane representation of an 8-bit image

Input: A gray scale image.
Output: Bit plane matrix and images.

Operation:
    Read the image.
    Read intensity values (G) from the Gray scale image.

    for i: 0 to 7
        for each pixel p do
            Find $bi \leftarrow i^{th}$ bit of G.
            Find $Ci \leftarrow bi *2^i$.
            Generate i^{th} Bit plane matrix using Ci.
        End
        Generate i^{th} Bit plane images.
    End

Algorithm. 1: Biplane

Fig 3.7 illustrate, an 8-bit image may be considered as being compose of eight 1-bit planes, with plane 1 containing the lowest order bit of all pixels in the image and plane 8 all the highest-order bit [21]. Bit plane slicing applies on the cover image and stego image of lena.bmp. Results are given below-

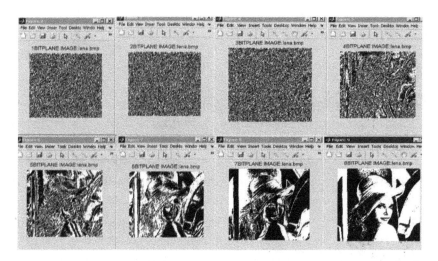

Fig 3.8 .Bit-plane slicing apply on cover image lena.bmp

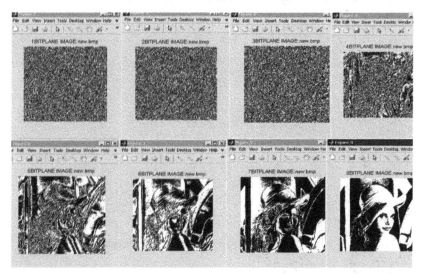

Fig 3.9. Bit-plane slicing is used on stego image Lena _stego.bmp

Observing two resulting biplanes, PVD values, histogram analysis where differences are not visible in normal perception. So, LSB based steganographic algorithm is successfully developed by us. It is clearly observable that we can embed m x n bits in m x n dimension gray image. Gray image is easily fit in describe procedure. We can assume a BMP is like a 3xGray image. So, above given model is implemented by us for BMP images.

3.1.3 High Embedded ratio obtained using LSB and Bitplane approach:

Internet is one of the medium of communication mostly used now a day. To conserve the security of information sent over the internet, steganographic concept makes its arrival. Least-significant bit and multi-bit embedding methods are the most well known and familiar in this domain. Here, in this work, only least-significant bit method is used. It is a new technique which is indeed very simple in comparison to the other existing ones in the sense that secret information is hidden inside the image. Here, we obtain an embedding ratio almost 8 times of the existing LSB algorithm by combining steganalysis tool 'bit-plane' and LSB algorithm applied over Gray-scale image. Estimated variance and standard deviation of stego-image is reduced here by deploying 'complement approach', LSB algorithm and bit-plane, which thereby enhances the quality of stego image. Hence, it is not possible for the intruder to extract content of the message sent by the user without using statistical approach (e.g.: correlation, standard deviation etc.)

Given information may be in complemented form is embedded in selected bit plane image. Compare between normal and complement information bit after insertion using LSB embedding algorithm [23]. Obtain standard deviation (S_d) for each image.

$$PVD = \left| (C_{i,j} - S_{i,j}) \right|.$$

$$S_d = \sum_{i=0,j=0}^{m,n} (C_{i,j} - S_{i,j})^2 / (m \times n).$$

Where,

[m,n]: is dimension of Gray scale image.

$C_{i,j}$: is intensity value at position (i,j) of cover image (before embedding).

$S_{i,j}$:is intensity value at position (i,j) of stego image(after embedding).

PVD: pixel value differencing

26

The used algorithms are given below-

Input: A gray image(C) and secret information (I_0).

Output: The Stego bit plane images, stego image (S) and S_d.

Operation:

    Read gray scale image.

    Call procedure Bitplane.

    Choose the ith (-1< i < 8) bitplane image where the text (I_0) is to be inserted.

    Call procedure ModifiedLsb.

    Call procedure CompModifiedLsb.

    Find pixel value differences (PVD) for each pixel of given gray scale image(C) and

        obtained stego image(S).

    Find Standard deviation (S_d) using PVD .

    Generate gray image using PVD value.

Algorithm. 2: Stegobitplane

First embedding algorithm based on normal or sequential LSB embedding algorithm [Algorithm. 3].Simply, LSB of bit planes are replaced by information bit sequences. Maximum difference (PVD) can be [-1, 0, 1], so for eight bit plane it can be [-8, 0, +8]. It is really hard to pick differences using normal vision.

Input: Chosen bitplane image and secret information (I_0).

Output: Embed and retrieve information from selected bitplane image.

Operation:

        Obtain bit sequence of I_0.

        Set LSB of bitplane image by sequence.

        Select LSB of the stego bitplane image.

        Retrieve the text.

Algorithm. 3: ModifiedLsb

27

If number of 1 s are more than 0s, then we will do complement of information sequence else normal LSB embedding. Our propose step really produces outstanding result [shows in Table II]. It shows PVD is reducing but effect (embedding & extraction) of algorithm is same. Algorithm is given below-

Input: Chosen bitplane image and secret information (I_0).
Output: Embed and retrieve information from selected bitplane image.

Operation:
  Obtain bit sequence of I_0.
  Obtain 1's Complement ($\overline{I_0}$) of bit sequence I_0.
  Count number of zeros (c_0) and ones (c_1) of I_0.
    If $c_0 > c_1$ then
      Call procedure ModifiedLsb.
    Else

      Set LSB of bitplane image by sequence($\overline{I_0}$).
      Select LSB of the stego bitplane image.
      1's complement of retrieve sequence.
      Retrieve the text.
  End

Algorithm . 4: CompModifiedLsb

o **Illustration of Algorithms with an example:**
Above given algorithms (Algorithm. 2, Algorithm. 3, Algorithm. 4) are applied on "new1.bmp" for same information and PVD value estimate, which is given below. The embedded information is retrieved at receiver side successfully. Both stego and cover are almost identical as lsb embedding changes the pixel values very negligible. Using pixel differencing values we can get detail analysis between two algorithms. Details of analysis are given below in pictorial format.

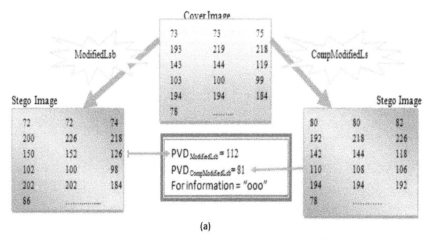

(a)

Fig 3.10. (a) PVD analysis using both algorithms for new1.bmp

It is one of the obtained results of my work, where pixel values of cover and stego images are given respectively. Calculate pixel differencing value (PVD) and other statistical parameters. All obtained results are analysis in result & discussion section, which will give in next section.

Algorithm. 2 is applied over several images, but for compeering purpose select image "new1.bmp" here. The Fig 3.10 (b) is shown below. Differences between the images are tough to get by normal vision.

Original Gray Scale Image	Stego Image using ModifiedLsb	Stego Image using CompModifiedLsb
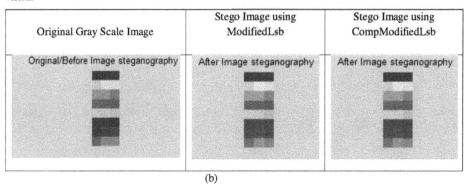		

(b)

Fig 3.10. (b) Stego images of new1.bmp using Algorithm 2

RESULT & DISCUSSION:

In Algorithm. 2, it is observed that it following normal LSB embedding [10]. But when takes an example, it exhibits embedding ratio is eight times of LSB embedding for each pixel. Consider "new1.bmp" to examine above statement:

Dimension of image (D) =[8,3].

Total number of pixel (P) =8X3=24.

Bits can embed using LSB method (E_{LSB}) =24

Embedding ratio (r_{LSB}) =24/24=1

For color image (RGB) embedding ratio= 1X3=3

Number of bit plane ($B_{1...7}$) =8

Embed bits using LSB method and Bitplane (E_{LSB}^{B}) =24 X 8=192

Embedding ratio (r_{LSB}^{B}) =E_{LSB}^{B}/ P =8 = 8 X (r_{LSB}).

So, above example shows that bitplane concept enhancing embedding ratio.

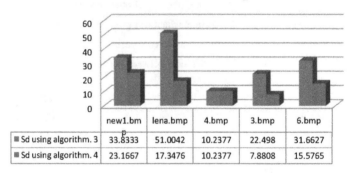

Standard Deviation (S$_d$)

	new1.bm	lena.bmp	4.bmp	3.bmp	6.bmp
■ Sd using algorithm. 3	33.8333	51.0042	10.2377	22.498	31.6627
■ Sd using algorithm. 4	23.1667	17.3476	10.2377	7.8808	15.5765

Table.3.3 : S$_d$ values

Thereby, we need to study high embedding ratio reflect any remarkable change in intensity values. So, Standard deviation (S$_d$) value estimate using both algorithm. 3 and algorithm. 4. In tabular format it is given above as table 3.3.

Above two algorithms have same embedding ratio (r_{LSB}^{B}) ,But S$_d$ value signifies using the algorithm. 4, we can get better result. Studying pixel value differencing (PVD) over original and stego image using both algorithm. 3 and algorithm. 4 and find position of change values. The Fig. 3.11 is shown below-

30

Name of image	Position of PVD using algorithm. 3	Position of PVD using algorithm. 4
new1.bmp		

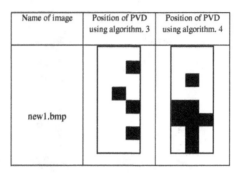

Fig. 3.11 Position of PVD

Position of change values in above Fig. 3.11, signifies that changes are more in number when applying algorithm. 4 and S_d values shows algorithm. 4 is better as compare algorithm. 3. Hence, we can conclude that algorithm. 4 is better than algorithm. 3.

Bitplane analysis [11][12] of "new1.bmp" using both two algorithms is given below in tabular format –

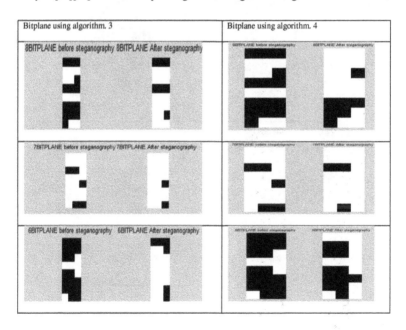

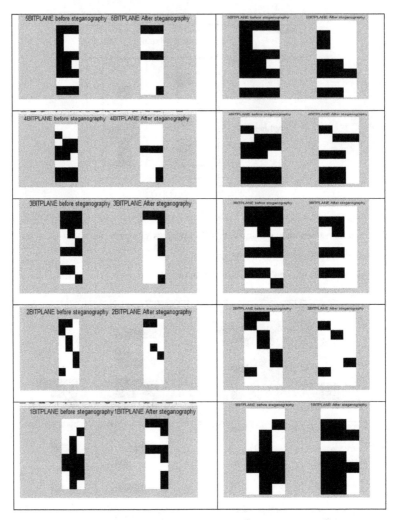

Table 3.4 : Bitplane($B_{8,7,...,1}$) using both algorithm. 3 and algorithm. 4

It is clearly visible in bitplane analysis that more positions of bitplane images are changed when applying Algorithm. 4 as compare with given algorithm. 3. At same time PVD calculation tells the success of algorithm .4.

32

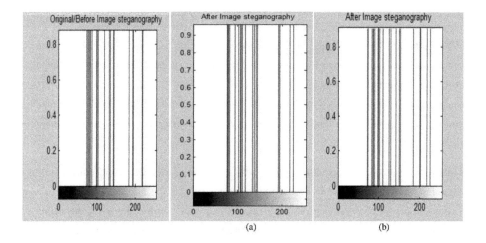

Fig . 3.12. (a) Histogram for cover and stego image using algorithm. 4 , (b) Histogram for cover and stego image using algorithm. 3

Bitplane analysis of stego and cover image of "new1.bmp" is clearly differentiate between both given algorithm. Histogram analysis [11][12] is also given for more detail level analysis. Histogram analysis is given in Fig . 3.12. (a) & (b). Computation vision (like Bit plane analysis, Histogram analysis, variance, standard deviation, correlations, PVD analysis etc) help to detect stego images.

Unlike lsb based embedding, multi bit steganographic algorithm helps to embed more than one bit information in each component of an image pixel with minimum distortion of image quality. So in simple lsb Steganography capacity evaluation (CE component [3.2.1]) is not important .But, at edge/boundary or in unsmooths (where color difference or pixel value difference is huge) region is more capable for embedding. So, CE component plays an important role in multi-bit embedding process.

While human perception is sensitive to huge change of pixel values, but small changes are never detected by human views. It is only detectable by human intelligent. To change in edge areas of pixels is more sensible from to change in smooth areas. To keep quality of image, we pay the attention to change pixel value from previous value by not much although multi-bit steganography principal is not altering any means.

Propose method describe in below section 3.2.1. In Section 3.2.1 we present our steganographic algorithm for gray-level images and bitmap images. Basic concept is taken from an exiting algorithm [7].

3.2.1. PROPOSED METHOD

UPPER-LEFT $P_{X-1,Y-1}$	UPPER $P_{X-1,Y}$	UPPER-RIGHT $P_{X-1,Y+1}$
LEFT $P_{X-1,Y}$	TARGET $P_{X,Y}$	

Fig. 3.13 A target pixel and its four neighboring pixels

Our system refers to four pixels adjacent to a target pixel in the embedding process

3.2.1.1 THE EMBEDDING OF SECRET INFORMATION

In this method, we have considered four neighboring pixels that have already finished embedding. Process to embed the secret message into the target pixel (refer to Fig.3.13) is given bellow:

Let, $P_{X,Y}$ is the target pixel (where to embed information) having intensity values $g_{X,Y}$. Let $g_{X-1,Y-1}$, $g_{X-1,Y}$, $g_{X-1,Y+1}$, $g_{X,Y-1}$ are the intensity values of pixel $P_{X-1,Y-1}$, $P_{X-1,Y}$, $P_{X-1,Y+1}$, $P_{X,Y-1}$ respectively which are the neighboring pixels of the target pixel $P_{X,Y}$ shown in fig 3.13 . If number of embedding bits is n and MSB of sequence is 0, then it provides better performance. The embedding procedure is as following:

Step 1.

Calculate the maximum (max) and the minimum (min) values among the four adjacent pixel values that are already embedded. Then calculate the difference value (d) between max & min values of pixels using the following formula:

Where:

$$g_{max} = max\{g_{X-1,Y-1}, g_{X-1,Y}, g_{X-1,Y+1}, g_{X,Y-1}\}\ldots\ldots \quad (1)$$
$$g_{min} = min\{g_{X-1,Y-1}, g_{X-1,Y}, g_{X-1,Y+1}, g_{X,Y-1}\}\ldots\ldots \quad (2)$$
$$d = g_{max} - g_{min} \ldots\ldots\ldots \quad (3)$$

Step 2.

Calculate the capacity evaluations (CE) of target pixel P(X,Y) ,It is the number of bit (n) of secret information can be inserted into target pixel of cover image.

$$n = \lfloor log_2^d \rfloor - 1 \qquad if\ d > 3$$
$$= 1 \qquad\qquad else \quad \ldots\ldots\ldots \quad (4)$$

If the value of d is less or equal to 3 then perform LSB embedding technique, otherwise value of n is taken from the result calculated using equation (4). We will enhance both the capacity and the quality/imperceptibility within the cover image.

Step 3.

Next to calculate a temporary value ($t_{x, y}$) using modulo operator that is sensing little bit change of pixel value:

$$t_{x, y} = b - (g_{xy} \bmod 2^n) \ldots\ldots\ldots\ldots \quad (5)$$

35

Where, b is the decimal representation of the hidden message using n bits.

Step 4.

To keep the quality of the image need to adjust temporary variable of cover image.

If $t_{x,y} \leq 2^{n-1}, Then:$

$$t'_{x,y} = \begin{cases} t_{x,y} & if \ \lfloor (2^{n-1})/2 \rfloor \leq t_{x,y} \leq \lceil (2^{n-1} - 1)/2 \rceil \\ t_{x,y} + 2^{n-1} & if \ (-2^{n-1} + 1) \leq t_{x,y} \leq \lfloor (2^{n-1})/2 \rfloor \\ t_{x,y} - 2^{n-1} & if \ \lceil (2^{n-1} - 1)/2 \rceil \leq t_{x,y} \leq 2^{n-1} \end{cases} \quad .....(6)$$

else

$$t'_{x,y} = t_{x,y} + q. \, 2^n \qquad where \ q \in \{-1, 0, +1\}$$

Consider the best option on the value of target pixel (the nearest value of $g_{x,y}$).

Step 5.

Finally, we calculate the new pixel value $g^*_{x,y}$ for target pixel P(X, Y) using:

$$g^*_{x,y} = g_{x,y} + t'_{x,y} \qquad .... \qquad (7)$$

Then we require to adjust, $g^*_{x,y}$ is outside-

$$g^*_{x,y} = \begin{cases} g^*_{x,y} + 2^n & if \ g^*_{x,y} < 0 \\ g^*_{x,y} - 2^n & if \ g^*_{x,y} > 255 \end{cases} \qquad .... \qquad (8)$$

3.2.1.2 THE EXTRACTION OF SECRET INFORMATION

Suppose the target pixel in stego image is $P^*_{X,Y}$ with pixel intensity value $g^*_{X,Y}$. Let $g^*_{X-1,Y-1}$, $g^*_{X-1,Y}$, $g^*_{X-1,Y+1}$, $g^*_{X,Y-1}$ are the pixel values of its upper-left $P^*_{X-1,Y-1}$ pixel, upper $P^*_{X-1,Y}$ pixel, upper-right $P^*_{X-1,Y+1}$ pixel, and left $P^*_{X,Y-1}$ pixel of target pixel, respectively.

Step 1.

Calculate the difference value d^* between the maximum pixel value and the minimum pixel value among the upper-left $P^*_{X-1,Y-1}$ pixel, upper $P^*_{X-1,Y}$ pixel, upper-right $P^*_{X-1,Y+1}$ pixel, and left $P^*_{X,Y-1}$ pixel.

$$g^*_{max} = max\{g^*_{X-1,Y-1}, g^*_{X-1,Y}, g^*_{X-1,Y+1}, g^*_{X,Y-1}\}\ldots\ldots\ldots \quad (9)$$

$$g^*_{min} = min\{g^*_{X-1,Y-1}, g^*_{X-1,Y}, g^*_{X-1,Y+1}, g^*_{X,Y-1}\}\ldots\ldots\ldots \quad (10)$$

$$d^* = g^*_{max} - g^*_{min} \ldots\ldots\ldots \quad (11)$$

Step 2.

Next calculate number (n) of insertion bits embedded in Target pixel during embedding process.

$$n = \lfloor log_2^{d^*} \rfloor - 1 \qquad if \ d^* > 3$$
$$=1 \qquad\qquad\quad else \qquad \ldots\ldots\ldots\ldots \quad (12)$$

Step 3. Calculating the value of b using:

$$b = mod(g^*_{X,Y}, 2^n) \ldots\ldots\ldots\ldots\ldots \quad (13)$$

The decimal value b is represented n bit binary sequence. We can see the secret message after completing the extraction processing.

EXAMPLE:

Case 1:

240	200	174
152	160	0
152	75	0

g_{max} =max{152,240,200,174}=240

g_{min}=min{152,240,200,174}=152

d=240-152=88

$n = \lfloor log_2^{88} \rfloor = 6$

But a maximum embeddable bit to a pixel is 5.

Suppose, information sequence 101110100 have to be embedded.

b=01110_2 =14_{10}

$t_{x,y} = 14 - (g_{xy} \bmod 2^{n-1})$

$\quad$ =14- (160 mod 16)

$\quad$ =14 -0

$\quad$ =14

$t_{x,y}$ belongs to higher level .So, adjustment is required.-

$g^*_{x,y} = 160 - 2 = 158$ $\qquad$ $t'_{x,y} = 14 - 2^4 = -2$

$g^*_{max} = max\{152,240,200,175\} = 240$

$g^*_{min} = min\{152,200,200,175\} = 152$

$d^*= 200 - 152 = 88$

$n = \lfloor log_2^{88} \rfloor - 1 = 5 - 1 = 4$

$b = mod(158, 2^4) = 14$

So, the new pixel value will be 158 instead of 174 (obtained in normal embedding).Even embedding using algorithm [7] gives the result for this case as 174 which is nearer to the actual pixel value(i.e.

38

160) of the cover image compare to embedding using the existing algorithm. Thus we can claim that our algorithm is more robust than the existing algorithm [7].

Case 2:

200	200	174
152	152	0
152	75	0

g_{max} =max{152,200,200,175}=200

g_{min} =min{152,200,200,175}=152

$d= |200 - 152| = 48$ $\qquad n = \lfloor log_2^{48} \rfloor = 5$

Suppose, information sequence 101110100 have to be embedded.

b= 01011_2 =11_{10}

$t_{x,y} = b - (g_{xy} \bmod 2^{n-1})$

$\qquad$ =11- (152 mod 16) [As, 15 <b< 0]

$\qquad$ =11-8=3 $\qquad t_{x,y}$ belongs to middle level .So, adjustment is not required.

$g^{*}_{x,y} = 152 + 3 = 155$

$g^{*}_{max} = max\{152,200,200,175\} = 200$
$g^{*}_{min} = min\{152,200,200,175\} = 152$

$d^{*}= 200 - 152 = 48$

$n = \lfloor log_2^{48} \rfloor - 1 = 5 - 1 = 4$

$b = mod(155, 2^4) = 11$

So, 11 will be embedded into target pixel 152. Here, changed pixel value is 3 but embedding bits is 4.Hence, it is increase the embedding ratio without distorting quality of image.

3.2.1.3 EXPERIMENT:

We have applied proposed multi-bit steganographic algorithm over several images and their stego images are given bellow respectively.

cubs24.bmp

stegocubs24.bmp

F3.bmp

stego F3.bmp

F2.bmp	stegoF2.bmp
F37.bmp	stegoF37.bmp

Fig 3.14.cover images (left side) and stego images (right side) obtained by applying proposed algorithm on cover images.

Number of embedding bits is calculated using (E_x) using total number of bits can be embedded into the each component(x) cover image according to algorithm. Embedding ratio (R_x) is the ratio of E_x and total number of pixels into a cover media. Variance (V_x) is ratio of square of PVD value and the count of pixel number. Table 3.14 gives the result of some statistical data like number of information bit, embedding ratio, and variance, etc for some of the tested 24-bit color images.

COVER IMAGE	DIMENSION	NUMBER OF PIXELS	RED EMBEDDING	GREEN EMBEDDING	BLUE EMBEDDING
cubs24.bmp	450X297	133650	$E_r=247383$ $R_r=1.8510$ $V_r=8.4435$	$E_g=247379$ $R_g=1.8509$ $V_g=9.2133$	$E_b=247380$ $R_b=1.8510$ $V_b=8.6682$
F3.bmp	280X210	58800	$E_r=162316$ $R_r=2.7605$ $V_r=15.6426$	$E_g=157768$ $R_g=2.6831$ $V_g=13.4437$	$E_b=177640$ $R_b=3.0211$ $V_b=40.9871$
F37.bmp	280X210	58800	$E_r=159178$ $R_r=2.7071$ $V_r=17.4623$	$E_g=156602$ $R_g=2.6633$ $V_g=13.0820$	$E_b=181170$ $R_b=3.0811$ $V_b=34.8932$
F2.bmp	280X210	58800	$E_r=177430$ $R_r=3.0175$ $V_r=16.2405$	$E_g=158958$ $R_g=2.7034$ $V_g=11.3053$	$E_b=221953$ $R_b=3.7747$ $V_b=54.5999$

Table 3.5. Embedded bits (E_x), Embedding ratio (R_x), variance (V_x) calculation for given images, where xϵ {red(r), green(g), blue(b)}

Table 3.5. shows that embedding ratio and embedding pixel values increases .The value of variance is low which proves robustness of our design steganographic algorithm.

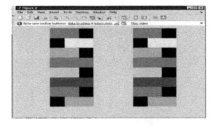

Fig. 3.15 .Cover image c.bmp and stegoc.bmp

Fig 3.15 represents the cover image and stego image. It is hard to differentiate between stego and cover image by normal vision.

3.2.1.3.A) PVD ANALYSIS

COLOR	PIXEL VALUE OF COVER IMAGE			PIXEL VALUE OF STEGO IMAGE		
RED	255	255	0	255	255	0
	0	255	255	1	248	252
	1	1	0	31	1	0
	254	254	254	254	252	255
	167	167	0	168	163	8
	129	129	129	129	128	134
	236	236	0	236	239	1
	0	1	1	1	8	4
GREEN	0	0	0	0	0	0
	0	255	255	8	255	225
	254	254	0	224	230	0
	1	1	1	2	6	3
	203	203	0	203	201	0
	65	65	65	66	68	63
	29	29	0	30	33	12
	0	182	182	0	179	184
BLUE	0	0	0	0	0	0
	0	0	0	8	8	0
	1	1	0	2	2	0
	254	254	254	255	224	230
	241	241	0	242	240	3
	1	1	1	1	1	0
	37	37	0	38	38	1
	0	238	238	1	240	238

Table 3.6. PVD values of cover image and different component of RGB model of stego image

Table 3.6. shows the maximum PVD is 30. But, mathematically the PVD lies in between 0 to 31. Higher PVD refers to the edge area of image. As in edge area the color difference between pixel and its neighboring pixel is very high so the difference of color levels (32 levels) may not be detectable for most of the images through naked eye.

B) HISTOGRAM ANALYSIS

Following figures help to analyze the histogram of a cover and a stego image before and after embedding the information into one of the sample images namely who.bmp and stegowho.bmp.

(a) cover image(before embedding)   (b) stego image(after embedding)

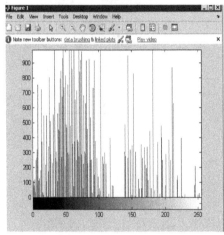 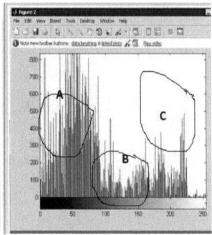

(c) Histogram analysis of cover image   (d) Histogram analysis of stego image

Fig 3.16. (a) F37.bmp(before embedding) (b) stegoF37.bmp(after embedding)
(c) and (d) Histogarm analysis of cover(F37.bmp) and stego image (stegoF37.bmp)

Both the cover and stego images and their histogram analysis are given above as in Fig 3.16. The differences are detected by three regions (A, B, C) as mark in histogram analysis. Similar to histogram analysis bit plane slicing also given below.

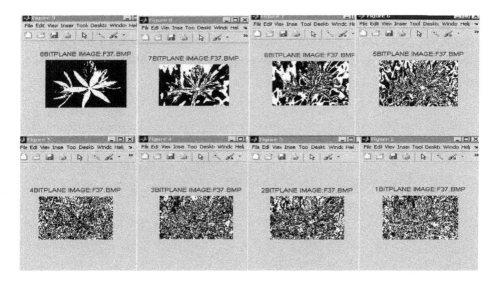

(a)

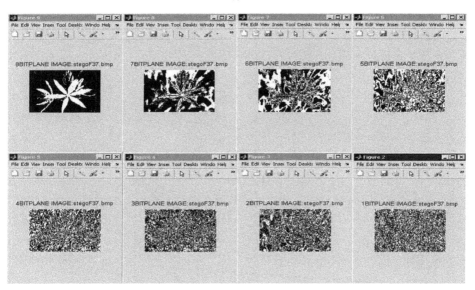

(b)

Fig. 3.17. (a)and (b) Bit-plane analysis of cover image and stego image of F37.bmp respectively

In above algorithm edge/boundary of cover image are remain unchanged. Other pixel values are studied for CE that enhances embedding capacity for cover image. Important here is the adjustment of temporary variable to get quality image even after steganography process. Hence, Algorithm is simpler to embed and extract.

3.2.2. Multi-Bit Embedding Adaptive Data Hiding in Edge Areas of Images Using Complement's Method:

Increasing embedding ratio to keep quality of image is always a challengeable task to researchers. Here the proposed method is to groom using wu et al's PVD, LSB replacement method and yang's *Adaptive data hiding in edge area of images with spatial LSB domain systems*. My proposed method reduces the pixel value differences almost 50% as compared to other existing algorithms with same embedding ratio. In my proposed work, 1's and 2's complement both can be applied on information bit sequences depending on the situation. All criterion and expected scenario are given with examples and analysis.

Calculate PVD for estimating capable embedding bits in pixel of an image and then obtain stego image without inferring image quality as compared to cover image. Difference of pixel value is categories in three range –lower level (LL), middle level (M.L) and higher level (H.L). PVD, No of enable embedding bits is represented by d and n respectively. Range of low level is (0 to 15), Middle level (16 to 31) and High level is (32 to 255), which is highlighted in Fig 3.18.

PVD Range	Diff. Value	n	◄lower level►◄middle level►◄ higher level──────►		
lower level	$0 \leq d \leq 15$	3	(0-15)	(16-31)	(32-255)
middle level	$16 \leq d \leq 31$	4			
higher level	$32 \leq d \leq 255$	5			

Fig. 3.18. PVD range and embedding bits in a pixel

If MSB =1 of capable embedding information bit, Then is complement it.

As per example: $A = 10011_2 = 19_{10}$ by 1's and 2's complement, we obtain. $\bar{A} = 01100_2 = 12_{10}$ and $\bar{A} + 1 = 01101_2 = 13_{10}$. So, both cases original bit stream is reduced in value while embedded. Proposed algorithm is given below-

Propose Method

$P_{x,y}$	$P_{x+1,y}$

Fig. 3.19. Two adjacent pixels

Suppose considering pixel $p_{x,y}$ and $p_{x+1,y}$ with value $g_{x,y}$ and $g_{x+1,y}$.

Embedding process is described bellow-

Step 1: calculate difference (d) of two adjacent pixels at positions (x, y) and (x+1, y) -

$$\text{Difference } (d_{x,y}) = |g_{x+1,y} - g_{x,y}|$$

Step 2: Estimate no of bits (n) capable in pixel $p_{x,y}$, $p_{x+1,y}$ using difference (d).

Step3: After calculating (n), select n bits from binary information. Suppose binary information is $b_{x,y}$.

If MSB of b is 1, then complement it, get b' and append 1 at end of $b_{x,y}$.

Else only append 0 at end of b

$$i_{x,y} = b'_{x,y}\underline{1} \text{ or } b_{x,y}\underline{0}$$

Here, underline 1 or 0 denotes, which binary sequence is complemented and which one not.

Situation provides to embed (n+1) bits to pixels of stego image. It is mandatory to be the $(n+1)^{th}$ bit is 0. So, don't care it. Intuitively, (n) no. of bits will be embedded in pixels of stego image in place of (n+1) bits [§].

Step4: Obtain change pixel value $g'_{x,y}$ and $g'_{x+1,y}$ using-

$$g'_{x,y} = g_{x,y} + i_{x,y}$$

$$g'_{x+1,y} = g_{x+1,y} + i_{x+1,y}$$

Where, $i_{x,y}$ and $i_{x+1,y}$: Capable embedded information with special LSB values

Step 5: In this step performing step 1 with change pixel values $g'_{x,y}$, $g'_{x+1,y}$. Calculate pixel-value-differencing (PVD) using modifies pixel vales, suppose it is d'$_{x,y}$.

$$\text{Then,} \quad \text{d'}_{x,y} = |g'_{x+1,y} - g'_{x,y}|$$

Step 6: If values of $d_{x,y}$ and d'$_{x,y}$ belong to different levels then require to readjustment.

Case 6.1. If $d_{x,y} \in$ lower level but d'$_{x,y} \notin$ lower level. Suppose d'$_{x,y}$ in middle level.

If $g'_{x+1,y} \geq g'_{x,y}$ then adjust $(g'_{x,y}, g'_{x+1,y})$ to being better choice between

$$(g'_{x,y} + 2^n, g'_{x+1,y}) \text{ and } (g'_{x,y}, g'_{x+1,y} - 2^n).$$

Else better choice between $(g'_{x,y} - 2^n, g'_{x+1,y})$ and $(g'_{x,y}, g'_{x+1,y} + 2^n)$.

Case 6.2.a. If $d_{x,y} \in$ middle level but $d'_{x,y} \in$ lower level. Then-

If $g'_{x+1,y} \geq g'_{x,y}$ then adjust $(g'_{x,y}, g'_{x+1,y})$ to being better choice between

$$(g'_{x,y}, g'_{x+1,y} + 2^n) \text{ and } (g'_{x,y} - 2^n, g'_{x+1,y}).$$

Else better choice between $(g'_{x,y} + 2^n, g'_{x+1,y})$ and $(g'_{x,y}, g'_{x+1,y} - 2^n)$.

Case 6.2.b. If $d_{x,y} \in$ middle level but $d'_{x,y} \in$ Higher level. Then-

If $g'_{x+1,y} \geq g'_{x,y}$ then adjust $(g'_{x,y}, g'_{x+1,y})$ to being better choice between

$$(g'_{x,y} + 2^n, g'_{x+1,y}) \text{ and } (g'_{x,y}, g'_{x+1,y} - 2^n).$$

Else better choice between $(g'_{x,y} - 2^n, g'_{x+1,y})$ and $(g'_{x,y}, g'_{x+1,y} + 2^n)$.

Case 6.3. If $d_{x,y} \in$ Higher level but $d'_{x,y} \notin$ Higher level.

If $g'_{x+1,y} \geq g'_{x,y}$ then adjust $(g'_{x,y}, g'_{x+1,y})$ to being better choice between

$$(g'_{x,y} - 2^n, g'_{x+1,y}) \text{ and } (g'_{x,y}, g'_{x+1,y} + 2^n).$$

Else better choice between $(g'_{x,y} + 2^n, g'_{x+1,y})$ and $(g'_{x,y}, g'_{x+1,y} - 2^n)$.

Else If values of $d_{x,y}$ and $d'_{x,y}$ belong to same levels then not require to readjustment.

Step 7: If $d_{x,y}$ and $d'_{x,y}$ are in same level then values of $(g'_{x,y}, g'_{x+1,y})$ remains unaltered.

Else continue Step 6.

Step 8: Embedding process is completed here.

Extraction process is also simpler one. That is-

Step 1: Calculate difference of two neighboring pixels to get their levels or calculate no. of embedded bits in a pixel of stego.

$$d^* = |g^*_{x+1,y} - g^*_{x,y}|$$

Step 2: Studying LSB of each pixels of stego images to obtain which binary sequence is to complement or which one not to.

Step 3: Selecting n bits to retrieves the hidden information. A Zero bit adds at beginning of (n) bits. So, total no of bits (n+1). According to LSB bit complement it if needed. Eventually, LSB bit is always 0. So, don't care it and retrieve n bits as secret information [§1].

[§]Given process perform during embedding secret information into pixels of cover Image. Suppose, $d_{x,y}$ signifies the PVD value of two adjacent pixels($p_{x,y}, p_{x+1,y}$) is in middle level. Value of n is 5.

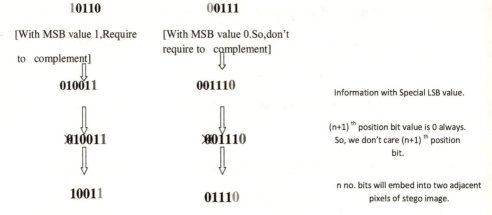

10110

[With MSB value 1,Require to complement]

⇩

010011

⇩

010011

⇩

10011

00111

[With MSB value 0.So,don't require to complement]

⇩

001110

⇩

001110

⇩

01110

Information with Special LSB value.

(n+1)th position bit value is 0 always. So, we don't care (n+1)th position bit.

n no. bits will embed into two adjacent pixels of stego image.

[§1] During extraction the PVD value (d^*) of two adjacent pixels ($p_{x,y}, p_{x+1,y}$) must lies in higher level by adjustment procedure (Step 6 in embedding). At then-

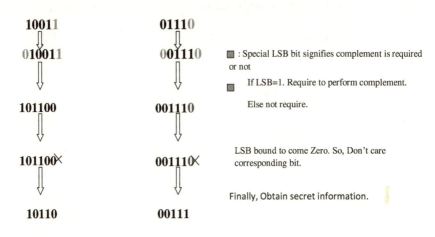

10011

⇩

010011

⇩

101100

⇩

101100✕

⇩

10110

01110

⇩

001110

⇩

001110

⇩

001110✕

⇩

00111

■ : Special LSB bit signifies complement is required or not

■   If LSB=1. Require to perform complement.

     Else not require.

LSB bound to come Zero. So, Don't care corresponding bit.

Finally, Obtain secret information.

In illustration of above propose method using few examples-

| 100 | 96 |

Given $g_{x,y}=100_{10}$ and $g_{x+1,y}=96_{10}$.

Difference $(d_{x,y})=|100 - 96| = 4$(lower level)

No. of embedding bits (n) =3 and Detecting LSB. So, Bits sequences

are: $C1\underline{1} = 0001_2$ and $C2\underline{1} = 001\underline{1}_2$. After don't care values are:

D1=001 and D2=011.

After embedding, the corresponding pixel values are-

$g'_{x,y} = 1100001_2 = 97_{10}$ and $g'_{x+1,y} = 1100011_2 = 99_{10}$.

So, MVD value after embedding is=2(lower level).

Selecting (n)=3 bits to decode hidden information.

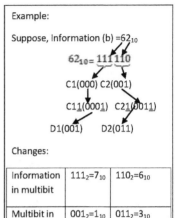

Example:

Suppose, Information (b) =62_{10}

$62_{10}=$ 111 110

C1(000) C2(001)

C1$\underline{1}$(0001) C2$\underline{1}$(0011)

D1(001)   D2(011)

Changes:

Information in multibit	$111_2=7_{10}$	$110_2=6_{10}$
Multibit in propose algorithm	$001_2=1_{10}$	$011_2=3_{10}$
reduce	6	3

% of reduce PVD =9/13X100= 70

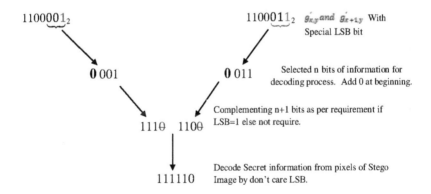

11000011_2 $g'_{x,y}$ and $g'_{x+1,y}$ With Special LSB bit

Selected n bits of information for decoding process. Add 0 at beginning.

Complementing n+1 bits as per requirement if LSB=1 else not require.

Decode Secret information from pixels of Stego Image by don't care LSB.

Above describing algorithm apply on $(15_{10}, 30_{10})$, $(30_{10}, 14_{10})$ for information 7_{10} , obtain result is quite satisfy our needs. It changes to $(16_{10}, 25_{10})$, $(32_{10}, 14_{10})$.Which is optimum one. We get best outcome from describe algorithm, when Step 7 of algorithm meet straight forward.

The forensic examiners use steganalysis more often, because steganographic algorithms are not known to the examiner then require to analysis stego image by steganalysis. Steganalysis is to break steganography. Steganalysis detector attempts to detect the presence of embedding massage when it is presented with in an image. Steganalysis is mainly classified in two categories [9]. Those are:

A. PASSIVE :
- Detect presence of hidden message in a stego image.
- If possible it is require retrieving steganographic algorithm.

B. ACTIVE:
- Estimate the embedded message length
- Location of hidden message
- Estimate parameters of steganographic algorithm.
- Extraction of hidden message

There is several existence algorithms on steganalysis, RS-Analysis is one of them; it is a non-sequential LSB embedding algorithm for digital images. It is also known as universal blind steganalysis Algorithm.

Here we are discussing about few algorithm in below. One of such algorithm [8], proposed by T. Zhang and X. Ping is based on the difference image histogram If dimension of the cover image(I) is M ×N with maximum data hiding capacity of LSB steganography is M ×N bits. Suppose, Maximum embedded capacity is e_m bits. But embedded bits is e_{em} .Then

Embedding ratio (p) is= $^{e_{em}}/_{e_m}$ x 100 ....   (1)

If, h_i : Difference image histogram

f_i: Reversing all the bits in LSB plane

g_i: After setting all the bits in LSB plane to zero

$a_{2i,2i+j}$: is define as the translation co-efficient from histogram g_i to h_i when j=0, 1,-1

It follows bellow properties:

- $0<a_{2i,2i+j}<1$ otherwise $a_{2i,2i+j}=0$

- $a_{2i,2i-1} + a_{2i,2i} + a_{2i,2i+1} = 1$ ....   (2)

Starting from the approximate symmetry about i=0 of difference image histogram, we get different translation co-efficient. In general, Image with the LSB plane fully embedded (p=100%) holds following properties-

$a_{2i,2i-1} \cong 0.25 \; ; a_{2i,2i} \cong .5 \; ; a_{2i,2i+1} \cong .25$

		$a_{2i,2i-1}$	$a_{2i,2i}$	$a_{2i,2i+1}$
	i=0	0.2316	0.5368	0.2316
Original	i=1	0.3115	0.5025	0.1860
	i=2	0.3527	0.4841	0.1632
	i=0	0.2451	0.5098	0.2451
p=50%	i=1	0.2805	0.5009	0.2186
	i=2	0.3025	0.4934	0.2041
	i=0	0.2503	0.4993	0.2503
p=100%	i=1	0.2502	0.5004	0.2494
	i=2	0.2508	0.5005	0.2487

Table 4.1: some translation coefficients

Let us denote,

$\alpha_i = a_{2i+2,2i+1} / a_{2i,2i+1}$

$\beta_i = a_{2i+2,2i+3} / a_{2i,2i-1} \cdots \cdots$ (3)

$\gamma_i = g_{2i} / g_{2i+2}$

For steganolytic methods for natural images, $\alpha_i = \gamma_i$

While for stego images with LSB plane fully embedded, we have $\alpha_i \approx 1$

For a given i the value of α_i decreases monotonously with the increase length of embedded secret message & embedding ratio reach to 100% , α_i decreases to 1 approximately.

Comparing lena.bmp for i=0

We model between α_i and embedding ratio p using quadratic polynomial $y = ax^2 + bx + c$ .Now we will discuss how to obtain value of p.

$c = \gamma_i$

$ap^2 + bp + c = \alpha_i$

$a(2-p)^2 + b(2-p) + c = \beta_i$...................... (4)

$a + b + c = 1$

Denote $d1 = 1 - \gamma_i$, $d2 = \alpha_i - \gamma_i$, $d3 = \beta_i - \gamma_i$

Then,

$2d1p^2 + (d3 - 4d1 - d2)p + 2d2 = 0$........... (5)

We can obtain embedding ratio p from root of equation. If discriminate of equation is smaller , the zero, we have $p \cong 1$

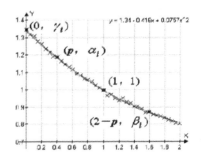

Fig 4.1. Functional relation between p and α

For various values of i, we can estimate the corresponding ratio of p and leads towards the average value   of final estimation of p.

Another famous approach is "Active Steganalysis using sequential stegranography" of Trivedi & R.chandramouli [9]. Sequential steganography as name implies embedded message in sequential manner or consecutive or successive samples. Cumulative sum (CUSUM) is derived for detecting the change point in observes stochastic process. Those are given below-

A. CUSUM FOR STEGANOLYSIS:

Suppose, the sequence of independent random variables of stego signal $\{y_k\}$ with pdf is $p_\theta(y)$, where θ can be a vector but use here as scalar quantity and θ can change after embedding a known value k. Log likelihood relation is:

$H_0: \theta = \theta_0$ when $k < k_0$ no embedded message from $k = 0$ to $k_0 - 1$

$H_1: \theta = \theta_1$ when $k \geq k_0$ embedded message start at location $k = k_0$ .... (6)

In this formulation three conditions may arise-

θ_0 and θ_1-are completely known .This case is arise for kercheoff's principal. The Stego algorithm is known. Only secret key is unknown.

θ_0 and θ_1- are partially known. A noisy estimation is possible. θ_0 and θ_1-may known from black box testing.

θ_0 and θ_1-are completely unknown, where the stego signal may available to steganalysis detector with no further information.

B. SEQUENTIAL PROBABILITY RATIO TEST (SPRT):

We consider CUSUM statistic (S_1^k), then equation (6) can be written in following form:

$$S_1^k = \sum_{i=1}^k S_i \begin{cases} \geq h & decide\ H_1 \\ < -\gamma & decide\ H_0 \\ k = k + 1\ otherwise \end{cases} \quad ....\ (7)$$

$S_i = \log(p_{\theta 1}(y_i)/p_{\theta 0}(y_i))$

h and γ are two threshold values. S_i give negative changes before tome k_0 and give positive change after it.

C. STEGENALYSIS OF SPREAD SPECTRUM EMBEDDING:

Suppose, stego image, cover image and embedded message carrier are y_k, x_k, w_k respectively. Corresponding message strength $\alpha > 0$.

Then we can write the equation like:

$$y_k = x_k + \alpha w_k \ where \ k = 1,2, \dots, N \ and \quad y_k \in R, x_k \in R, w_k \in R \ \dots\dots(8)$$

If message length <N, Then $\alpha = 0$ for the corresponding indices,

If $\quad x_k \sim N(0, \sigma_0^2)$

$\quad w_k \sim N(0, \sigma_1^2)$

$\quad y_k \sim N(0, \sigma_0^2 + \sigma_1^2)$

If message is embedded from k_0 to k_1 then-

$$y_k \sim \begin{cases} N(0, \sigma_0^2) \ where \ k = 1 \ to \ k_0 - 1 \\ N(0, \sigma_0^2 + \sigma_1^2) \ where \ k = k_0 \ to \ k_1 \dots\dots\dots\dots (9) \\ N(0, \sigma_1^2) \ where \ k = k_1 + 1 \ to \ N \end{cases}$$

So, above steps are mentions here. They will calculate embedded message length in cover image and embedding ratio.

Now a day's, concepts of classifier also introduce to identify cover or stego images. Machine intelligence or artificial intelligence concept is required to cluster the testing image properly. Basic concept is given below.

- ❖ Considering any one of the features in spatial or frequency domain of testing image
- ❖ Set the threshold value of the classifier based on the features.
- ❖ Extracted features of testing image are comparing with threshold value.
- ❖ Classifier will cluster the testing image into stego or cover.

Several algorithms are present right now. One of them is Jun, Hu, Yuan's classifier concept. How a classifier is work, it is shown below using Fig. 4.2.

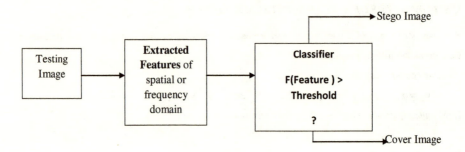

Fig. 4.2 Classifier to identify stego or cover image

We can use the image sterilization technique in image processing to destroy any steganographic information as much as possible so that the pixel values of the output image at a particular position is almost alike to that of the corresponding cover image.

5.1. Double Bit Sterilization of Stego Images

We extend the idea to sterilize two least significant bits of pixel intensities. The technique does not need to know how the information has been embedded inside the image. We performed extensive experiments over stego images created by multibit steganography algorithm and our technique succeeded in sterilizing around 77% of stego pixels on average (with a maximum of 99%).

We devise a neighborhood-based multi-bit sterilization technique in spatial domain by altering the pixel values as minimum as possible. The method consists of two rules, namely, the Selection Rule and the Substitution Rule.

A) SELECTION RULE:

This rule specifies how to select the pixels whose values would be modified by the sterilization algorithm.

Rule:1

Selection Rule 1 is valid for 1st row of pixel values except the top-left and the top-right corner position.

	$P_{i,j}$	$P_{i,j+1}$
$P_{i+1,j-1}$	$P_{i+1,j}$	$P_{i+1,j+1}$

Select the LSBs of two adjacent pixels $P_{i+1,j-1}$ and $P_{i+1,j}$ and make a bit sequence b_x of length two. Similarly, select the LSBs of the other two adjacent pixels $P_{i+1,j+1}$ and $P_{i,j+1}$ to make another bit sequence b_y of the same length.

Rule:2

Selection Rule 2 is applied when the target pixel is present at the last row of the stego image except the bottom-left and the bottom-right positions.

$P_{i-1,j-1}$	$P_{i-1,j}$	$P_{i-1,j+1}$
$P_{i,j-1}$	$P_{i,j}$	

Select the LSBs of two adjacent pixels $P_{i-1,j+1}$ and $P_{i-1,j}$ and make a bit sequence b_x of length two. Similarly, select the LSBs of the other two adjacent pixels at $P_{i-1,j-1}$ and $P_{i,j-1}$ to make another bit sequence b_y of the same length.

Rule:3

Selection Rule 3 is applicable for the target pixel at the top-left corner.

$P_{i,j}$	$P_{i,j+1}$
$P_{i+1,j}$	$P_{i+1,j+1}$

Select the LSBs of two adjacent pixels $P_{i+1,j}$ and $P_{i+1,j+1}$ and make a bit sequence b_x of length two. Similarly select the LSB of the right pixel $P_{i,j+1}$ and consider 0 (since no other adjacent pixel is available) to make another bit sequence b_y of the same length.

Rule:4

Selection Rule 4 is applied when the target pixel is at the bottom-left corner of the image.

$P_{i-1,j}$	$P_{i-1,j+1}$
$P_{i,j}$	$P_{i,j+1}$

Select LSBs of two adjacent pixels $P_{i-1,j}$ and $P_{i-1,j+1}$ and make a bit sequence b_x of length two. Similarly, select LSB of the right pixel $P_{i,j+1}$ of target pixel and consider 0 (since no other adjacent pixel is available) to make another bit Sequence b_y of the same length.

Rule:5

Selection Rule 5 is used when the target pixel is at top right corner of the image.

$P_{i,j-1}$	$P_{i,j}$
$P_{i+1,j-1}$	$P_{i+1,j}$

Select the LSBs of the two adjacent pixels $P_{i+1,j-1}$ and $P_{i+1,j}$ and make a bit sequence b_x of length two. Similarly, select the LSB of the left pixel $P_{i,j-1}$ and consider 0 (since no other adjacent pixel is available) to make another bit sequence b_y of the same length.

Rule:6

Selection Rule 6 can be used when position of target pixel is at the bottom right corner of the image.

$P_{i-1,j-1}$	$P_{i-1,j}$
$P_{i,j-1}$	$P_{i,j}$

Select the LSBs of two adjacent pixels $P_{i-1,j-1}$ and $P_{i-1,j}$ and make a bit sequence b_x of length two. Similarly, select the LSB of the left pixel $P_{i,j-1}$ and consider 0 (since no other adjacent pixel is available) to make another bit sequence b_y of the same length.

B) PROCESSING AND SUBSTITUTION:

Step 1:

Perform bit-wise XOR operation between the two bit sequences of length two as follows.

$$r_z \leftarrow b_x \oplus b_y$$

Step2:

Get the last two bits of the target pixel intensity and refer it as b_z. Perform bit-wise AND operation of b_z with the complement r'_z of r_z to get r''_z.

$$r''_z \leftarrow r'_z \,\&\, b_z$$

Step-3:

Substitute the two LSBs of the target pixel with r''_z.

Input: A stego-image.
Output: Sterilized image.
Operation:
Read the intensity values of the stego image.
for each pixel do
    Choose the appropriate rule to make the
        bit sequence.
        for each adjacent bit sequence do
           (i)Perform bitwise XOR .
           (ii) Perform bitwise AND between the
                2 LSB of the target pixel.
        end
end
Output the transformed image.
	Input: A stego-image.
	Output: Sterilized image.
	Operation:
	Read the intensity values of the stego image.
	for each pixel do
	        counter++;
	        if ((p =counter%2) == 0)
	           Choose the LSB of each pixel
	           if(LSB==0) LSB=1
	           else LSB=0
	           end
	        end
	end
	Output the transformed image.

Algorithm : Double Bit Sterilization	**Algorithm : Sequential LSB Sterilization**

C) EXPERIMENTAL RESULT

To estimate the accuracy of our technique, we need to take as inputs some sample stego images for which we know which pixel values are actually changed due to the double bit embedding. Let S be the number of stego pixels and S' out of those S pixels actually differ in intensity values when compared with the corresponding cover image. Now, suppose S" out of those S' pixels are recovered due to the sterilization process. By recovery, we mean at least one of the two least significant bits is recovered. We calculate the accuracy of double bit sterilization for this image as S"=S'. We have used a database of 150 different 24-bit color images in BMP format and 100 gray-scale images (downloaded from internet). We have also prepared different text files containing the story of Evidence (downloaded from [22]). We have used MATLAB 7.7.0 as a software tool for implementation. We have applied the above algorithm on stego images to obtain their sterilized versions. Histogram and Pixel Value Difference (PVD) analysis are shown in tabular format in the following subsections, where it is clearly obtained that maximum PVD value change lies in between -3 to +3. We find that almost 77% to 99% of stego information has been destroyed without distorting the quality of image. In Table 5.1 & 5.2, we show the performance of our sterilization algorithm on two multi-bit steganography algorithms. Algorithm A refers to ordinary sequential embedding, whereas algorithm B refers to the technique of [23].

Histogram Analysis:

The main purpose to analyze the histogram [21] is to detect significant changes in the frequency of occurrence of each color component in an image by comparing the sterilized image with the stego image. Fig 5.1 is showing the histograms of one bmp image and its sterilized version.

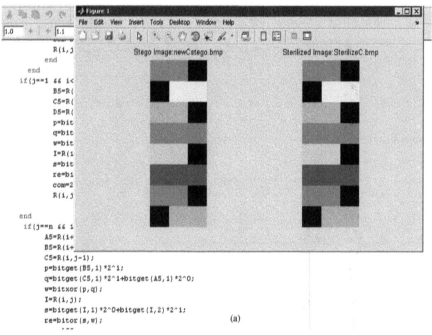

(a)

Stego image (newCstego.bmp)			Sterilize image (sterilizeC.bmp)		
255	255	0	252	252	0
0	255	255	0	252	252
1	1	0	0	0	0
254	254	254	252	252	252
167	167	0	164	164	0
129	129	129	128	128	128
236	236	0	236	236	0
0	1	1	0	0	0

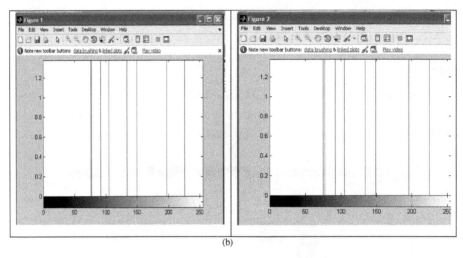

(b)

Fig 5.1 (a) Experimental results between stego (newCstego.bmp) and sterilize (sterilizeC.bmp) images (b) PVD and histogram.

The **Pixel Value Difference** (PVD) is determined by:

$$PV\,D_{i,j} = |\,C_{i,j} - S_{i,j}\,|\,;$$

Where $C_{i,j}$ is the pixel value of the red component of the cover image at the (i, j)-th position and $S_{i,j}$ is the pixel value of the red component of the stego image at the (i, j)-th position. Fig 5.1 show that the PV $D_{i,j}$, thus changes in pixel intensity values between both images.

... ale usual m...
...ple hurrying for the o...
traffic on the road. Therefore i
was quite crowded and compact,
excluding a police vehicle which rushed
through the crowd. The atmosphere
around became tense, as the vehicle
was rushing with its ear splitting
siren sound. The crowd on the
road split immediately to provide a
way through. The ones who were
walking on the footpath were looking
back at the departing vehicle with
curious, fearful expressions on their
faces. As the vehicle departed it
left a notion of tension on the road
for a while yet things gradually
returned to normality.

Embeded Messege [2] using [5] before Sterilization

⇩

Vjfrd!wcp"tjg‡ tptao‡ ommjmd
‡ stqk/!rfosmd!hvpp{jlg‡ gls tjg"
neekbe."usbeeia"mm thf pnbg/ Vhgpg
emse‡ hv!ucs‡ pwiuf!bmvdfg‡
hnd‡ 'oor"t.‡ dybotghnd‡ ' pmmicd
ugkj'od"uhkaj qvpiee vjmuek tie‡ crnue/‡
Vjg 'umnssjerg‡ bsowmg‡
cfb'le‡ wdlrf-!ap"whd"tfhjamg"v's
pwpiknd wjuk‡ hwr!gbr‡ rsljvvkod
skqen!qlumf-‡ Vkg cplvf‡
ml"wje‡ smaf"rqniw"inledha
ueoz ul‡ rpouhdd '"ubx‡
vipovdh. Wkd‡ onfs‡ wil!tfqd
‡ waokhlf!mm‡ tkg‡ elm
us'vk"udpf"innhkle cb'i cu thd
egsarvkod!udjhamg!vhvi"cwrhluq
.!gecqgwo d{qsgsqklnr‡ oo!tjghq dabfs.!
Ap!whd‡ tgkjblg"fdqcpufe‡
'!deu!c mmtknn!mf!udmqjml"lo wke'
'f gos!c vjkog!xfw‡ uhjnfr‡
...!‡ qdtvsodg"tm!on...

Table 5.1: Sample text [22] embedded in an image before and after sterilization

Accuracy (minimum, maximum, average) of sterilization over 100 gray-scale and 150 color images for two different algorithms A and B.

A-sequential LSB sterilization   B-Double bit sterilization Algorithms

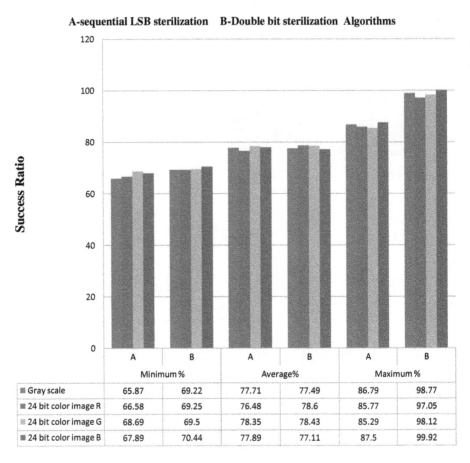

	Minimum %		Average%		Maximum %	
	A	B	A	B	A	B
Gray scale	65.87	69.22	77.71	77.49	86.79	98.77
24 bit color image R	66.58	69.25	76.48	78.6	85.77	97.05
24 bit color image G	68.69	69.5	78.35	78.43	85.29	98.12
24 bit color image B	67.89	70.44	77.89	77.11	87.5	99.92

Table 5.2 Successful sterilization ratio

Fig 5.2 is shown that we can retrieve more pixel values from unchanged stego image using sterilization method. Sterilization method is not only used for destroying steganographic algorithm, it can also used to retrieve cover image. So, it is clearly signifies our algorithm is more robust.

Fig 5.2 cover image, stego image and sterilize images for images (F3.bmp, F37.bmp, F36.bmp)

CE: Capacity of Embedding
IGSC: improved gray-scale compensation
LSB: Least Significant bit
MER: Minimum-error replacement
MSB: Most Significant bit
MULTI-BIT: Multiple bit
PVD: Pixel value differencing
PDF: Probability density function
3D: Three Dimension

[1] N. Huang, M. Li, and C. Wang -" Toward Optimal Embedding Capacity for Permutation Steganography"- Member, IEEE.

[2] F. Huang, B. Li, J. Huang-"Attack Lsb Matching Steganography By Counting Alteration Rate Of The Number of Neighbourhood Gray Levels"- 2007 IEEE.

[3] A. Bogomjakov, C. Gostman, and M. Isenburg - "Distortion-free steganography for polygonal meshes,"- Comput. Graph. Forum, vol.27, no. 2, pp. 637–642, 2008.

[4] Y. K.Leea and L.H. Chena. "High capacity image steganographic model" -IEE Proc. -Vis. Image Signal Process., Vol. 147, No. 3, June 2000 IEE Proceedings . online no. 20000341.

[5] H. C. Wu, N. I. Wu, C. S. Tsai, and M. S. Hwang, "Image steganographic scheme based on pixel-value differencing and LSB replacement methods," Proc. Inst. Elect. Eng., Vis.Images Signal Process.,vol. 152, no. 5, pp. 611–615, 2005.

[6] C. Yang, C.Weng, S. Wang-" Adaptive Data Hiding in Edge Areas of Images With Spatial LSB Domain Systems", IEEE, and Hung-Min Sun.

[7] Y.Park, H.Kang, S.Shin, and K. Kwon. Y. Hao et al. (Eds.)- "An Image Steganography Using Pixel Characteristics"- CIS 2005 Part II, LNAI 3802, pp.581 – 588, 2005.© Springer-Verlag Berlin Heidelberg 2005.

[8] T. Zhang, X.Ping -"Reliable detection of LSB Steganography based on the difference Image histogram"-Department of Information Science, University of Information Engineering,Zhengzhou ,P.R.China.

[9] S. Trivedi and R.Chandramouli -"Active Steganalysis of Sequential Steganography" Multimedia Systems, Communication and Networking (MSyNC) Laboratory Electrical and Computer Engineering,Stevens Institute of Technology.

[10] J. Fridrich, M. Goljan, R. Du-" Lossless Data Embedding For All Image Formats"- Department of Electrical Engineering, SUNY Binghamton, Binghamton, NY 13902.

[11] G. Paul, I. Mukherjee –" Image Sterilization to Prevent LSB-based on the steganographic transmission "- Member, IEEE.

[13] G.C.Kessler-http://www.garykessler.net/library/crypto.html.

[14] "Steganography Techniques"- infosyssec.com/.../techniques.htm.

[15] "- J. Cummins, P.Diskin, S.Lau and R. Parlett, " Steganography And Digital Watermarking School of Computer Science, The University of Birmingham.

[16] "http://en.wikipedia.org/wiki/Julius_Caesar" secret information.

[17] "http://sarc-wv.blogspot.com", forensic examiner.

[18] C.C. Chang , H.W. Tseng: "A Steganographic Method for Digital Images Using Side Match, Pattern Recognition Letters", ELSEVIER, Vol. 25, June (2004) 1431-1437.

[19] C.C. Thien , J.C. Lin: "A Simple and High-Hiding Capacity Method for Hiding Digit-by-Digit Data in Images Based on Modulus Function", The Journal of The Pattern Recognition Society, PERGAMON, Vol. 36,June (2003) 2875-2881.

[20] F. Huang, B. Li, J. Huang-" Attack Lsb Matching Steganography By Counting Alteration Rate Of The Number Of Neighbourhood Gray Levels"- Dept. of Electronics and Communication Engineering,Sun Yat-Sen University, Guangzhou, Guangdong, 510275, P. R. China.

[21] R.C.Gonzalez "Digital image processing"-Prentice Hall publication.

[22] www.englishnovels.net/2008/04/ch-2-evidence-free-novels-aghast.html

[23] Y. Park, H. Kang, S. Shin and K. Kwon. An Image Steganography Using Pixel Characteristics. In International Conference on Computational Intelligence and Security (CIS 2005), pages 581-588, vol. 3802, Lecture Notes in Computer Science, Springer.

[24] A. Bogomjakov, C. Gotsman, and M. Isenburg, "Distortion-free steganography for polygonal meshes," Eurographics, vol. 27, no. 2, pp. 637-642, 2008.